# Why Is Mass Important?

## Mass Is Special!

Did you know that going to Mass is one of the most special things you can do for yourself, your family, and friends? At Mass, Catholics work to become the people God wants us to be.

**We go to Mass to:**

- thank God for everything he has given us;
- learn more about God and how he wants us to live;
- remember that Christ died to save us from sin and death;
- receive Christ in the **Eucharist** so he can live inside us and make us more like him;
- be sent out to live what Christ taught and to share that with others.

  This book will help you learn to love the Mass by showing how you can be an active part of the Mass and not just someone who sits and watches it take place.

Christ is really at Mass!

1

## Mass Is Where We Meet Christ

Going to Mass is so important that the Church wants every Catholic to go, especially on Sundays (or Saturday night)—and on **Holy-days of Obligation**. Sometimes you may even attend Mass during the week. No matter when you go, everything you do at home, at school, or at play during your week is made more holy by what you hear, say, eat, and drink at Mass. Why? Because we meet Christ in every Mass.

### Christ is present at Mass in four ways:

1. In the Eucharist
2. In the priest
3. In the Word of God
4. In the people

## We All Participate at Mass

When we gather for Mass, we are not an audience, watching the priest and **ministers** "do" the Mass. It is what we all do together. You have a special part in that holy work. We call that **participation**—being part of the action. Think about it. If you are on a sports team, you'd rather play than sit on the bench, right? If you are in a band or a choir, you want to make music.

If you are at a party, you want to be part of the fun.

You are part of the Mass when you sing, listen, say the **responses**, and pray. When every-

### Reflect and Share

Choose one of the four ways Christ is present at Mass and tell your parents why you think it is important.

one in church puts their voices together, it makes one big sound of God's people praying. When we praise God, we join the crowd cheering for the "winning team." Just like your team or group needs you to be at its best, your Church community needs your voice at Mass. Don't be left out!

## Pray with Your Whole Body

To be fully a part of Mass, you should also pray with your whole self. With our bodies, we make the **Sign of the Cross**, stand, sit and kneel, and walk to the altar to receive **Communion** (Eucharist). If, because of disability, you are not able to do it all, do what you can in your own best way.

## We Listen, Speak, Believe, and Live as God's People

Listen with your whole heart at Mass. Why? If you let him, God can use the prayers, readings, and the Eucharist to make you a better, more loving person — someone who is not selfish but who helps others in the name of Christ.

You don't do this alone. When you were baptized, you became part of God's family, the Church. Say your responses along with everyone else. Why? Because everything we pray at Mass is what we believe together. The faith we share at Mass shapes how we as Catholics live together as God's holy people, working to make a better world.

## Prayer Activity

Close your eyes and remember something about Mass that feels holy or special. Write a sentence or two, or draw a picture in the space below to show this. Sit quietly and thank God in your heart.

## Pray with Your Family:

Dear God,
you sent your Son to offer his life for us
and to tell us to remember him in the Mass.
We thank you for Christ in the Eucharist.
We thank you for our priests, who help us see Christ.
We thank you for letting us be your people and for
   your love for us.
Make us more holy by the work we do at Mass.
Through Christ our Lord.
Amen.

## To Do This Week

Next time you are at Mass, join in singing the songs and saying your responses. If you still need to learn some of the parts of the Mass, just do your best. God wants to hear you!

## Family Connection

- Discuss how you can make Sunday Mass a special part of your weekend family time.

- Sit down together with the family calendar and plan when you can go to Mass. Be flexible. You may attend a different Mass each weekend in order to accommodate your busy schedules. If you will be out of town, look on the Internet for a Catholic church near where you plan to be. Mark the time and place on the calendar. Plan to do this at the beginning of every month.

- Think about your own childhood experience of attending Mass. Did you attend Mass with your family? What do you remember most about that? How can you make the experience of Mass "friendlier" for your child? Talk about this with your child.

# Chapter 2

## We Get Ready for Mass

### Preparing Yourself

Think about how you get ready for other events by doing the activity at the bottom of page 7. Compare this to going to Mass. Mass is a special event too. You are going to meet Christ! We get ourselves ready for Mass on both the outside and on the inside.

**On the outside, you show respect to God and other people at church by doing these things:**

> **FUN FACT**
> We fast before Mass so that Christ will fill us!

- Be sure you are clean — especially your hands — to receive Communion.

- Dress in clean clothes that are appropriate for going to church. Ask your parents to help you choose suitable clothing.

- Do not eat anything (including chewing gum) for one hour before Mass. You may drink water.

- **Genuflect** as you enter church if the **tabernacle** is in the room. (Christ is present in the tabernacle.) If the tabernacle is not near the altar you bow to the altar.

- Be friendly to other worshippers, but quiet as you wait for Mass to start. It is best not to disturb people who are praying.

**You can get ready on the inside by doing these things:**

- Look at the readings you will hear at Mass ahead of time.

- Think, pray, and talk about the readings at school, religious education class, or with your family.

- Think of someone or something that needs your prayer. This is your personal **intention** for the Mass.

- Sign yourself with holy water as you enter the church to remind you of your Baptism.

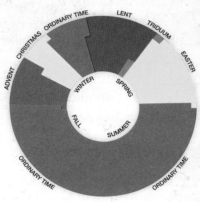

- Notice which **season** of the **liturgical year** it is. Look at how the church has been decorated and the color the priest wears.

- Pray before Mass starts. (Use the kneeler if there is one.)

When you are invited to a party or special event, how do you get ready?

## The People Get Ready

Even before Mass begins, ministers have been getting ready. Musicians have practiced the songs ahead of time. **Readers** have practiced their readings. **Sacristans** and **altar servers** have put out the bread and wine, the special cloths, and **vessels** the priest will use during the Mass. **Hospitality** ministers have greeted and welcomed people. Everyone has found a seat and prayed before Mass starts.

## Introductory Rites

Before we can hear the Word of God, we need a special way to get the ministers of the Mass into place. We also need to prepare ourselves to begin listening to God by asking forgiveness, praising and thanking him for all he has done for us. This first part of the Mass is called the **Introductory Rites**.

### Opening Procession

Mass begins with a **procession**, a kind of "parade" to the altar. A server who carries a special **processional cross** goes first, followed by other altar servers, a deacon or reader carrying the *Book of the Gospels*, and the priest who will lead the Mass.

As Mass begins, the song leader, or **cantor**, invites everyone to stand and sing the **opening song**. It's time to find the words and music in the hymnal, songbook, or **worship aid**. As the music begins, it is your turn to sing, too.

Watch as the ministers get close to the altar. The reader and altar servers bow to the altar before taking their places. The priest and deacon, if there is one, walk around behind the altar and kiss it. They are reverencing the altar, which represents Christ. Sometimes, if this is a special occasion, the priest may bless the altar with **incense**, a sweet-smelling smoke made by burning a special mixture in a **censer**.

## Saying Hello in a Special Way

As the song ends, the priest and all the people make the Sign of the Cross and we put ourselves in the presence of Christ as the priest greets us with one of three sentences that come from the Bible:

> **"The grace of our Lord Jesus Christ,**
> **and the love of God,**
> **and the communion of the Holy Spirit**
> **be with you all."**

> **"Grace to you and peace from God our Father**
> **and the Lord Jesus Christ."**

> **"The Lord be with you."**

The priest's greeting recognizes that Christ is present within us. We answer: **"And with your spirit."** This says that we know the priest has a special role as our leader. During Mass, he acts in the place of Christ.

## Asking Forgiveness

Before we can be worthy to worship God, we must first ask him to forgive our sins, because we sometimes fail him. In his love and mercy, God waits for us to try again to live his way. We approach

God humbly in the **Penitential Act** to ask for forgiveness and help. The priest invites us: **"Brothers and sisters, let us acknowledge our sins, and so prepare . . ."** Then we think about our sins in a moment of silence. Next, we say the Penitential Act together. We do this in one of these three ways:

## Option 1

# The Confiteor

I confess to almighty God
and to you, my brothers and sisters,
that I have greatly sinned,
in my thoughts and in my words,
in what I have done and in what I have
   failed to do,

And, striking their breast, they say:

through my fault, through my fault,
through my most grievous fault;

Then they continue:

therefore I ask blessed Mary ever-Virgin,
all the Angels and Saints,
and you, my brothers and sisters,
to pray for me to the Lord our God.

## Option 2

| Priest: | Have mercy on us, O Lord. |
| --- | --- |
| **People:** | **For we have sinned against you.** |
| Priest: | Show us, O Lord, your mercy. |
| **People:** | **And grant us your salvation.** |

## Option 3

*In this option the deacon or cantor may sing or say three verses that are directed to Christ and the wonderful things he has done for us. We respond with a simple phrase, an **invocation**, about Christ's loving mercy.*

**Priest/Deacon:** You were sent to heal the contrite of heart: Lord, have mercy. / *Kyrie, eleison.*

**People:** Lord, have mercy / *Kyrie, eleison.*

**Priest/Deacon:** You came to call sinners: Christ, have mercy. / *Christe, eleison.*

**People:** Christ, have mercy. / *Christe, eleison.*

**Priest/Deacon:** You are seated at the right hand of the Father to intercede for us: Lord, have mercy. / *Kyrie, eleison.*

**People:** Lord, have mercy. / *Kyrie, eleison.*

## Kyrie

If we didn't already say it (look at option 3 above), we then say or sing the **Kyrie.** The Kyrie is a **litany,** a series of repeated **petitions** directed to Christ. The priest, deacon or cantor invites: **"Lord, have mercy"** (or *Kyrie, eleison*), **"Christ, have mercy"** (or *Christe, eleison*) and finally, **"Lord, have mercy"** (or *Kyrie, eleison*). We repeat each one. The petition is actually a joyful text; it recognizes that Christ rose from the dead and pleads for us to God the Father.

After one of these three options is prayed, the priest offers the absolution. This is not the same as going to the Sacrament of Reconciliation.

11

The absolution asks for God's forgiveness on everyone who is present: **"May almighty God have mercy on us, forgive us our sins, and bring us to everlasting life."** We reply: **"Amen,"** because it affirms our belief in the love and mercy of God.

## Sprinkling Rite

Sometimes, instead of the Penitential Act, we remember our Baptism with the **Sprinkling Rite**. This usually happens during **Easter Time**. The priest carries an **aspersorium** (special bucket) and sprinkles holy water on the people using an **aspergillum**, a wand or branch, to shake the water.

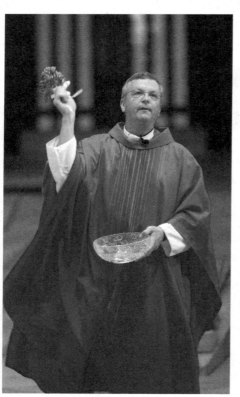

> ### FUN FACT
> Did you know that *Kyrie, eleison* and *Christe, eleison* are in the Greek language?

## Praising God: The Gloria

Next, (except during **Advent** or **Lent**) we sing the **Gloria**— the song the angels sang to the shepherds when Christ was born: **"Glory to God in the highest, and on earth peace to people of good will."** In this song, we praise and thank God the Father, Son, and Holy Spirit.

## Reflect and Share

Talk with your parents about why you think we tap our chests with our fist at the words: "through my fault, through my fault, through my most grievous fault"?

## The Collect

The priest says: **"Let us pray."**
In the brief silence that follows, remember your personal intention for the Mass. The priest then reads from a special book, called *The Roman Missal*, held for him by an altar server. This special prayer is called the **Collect** because it "collects" all of our silent intentions. It also helps us know more about the

season, the Sunday, or if the Mass is on another special day. After the Collect, we sit down to listen to the Word of God in the **Liturgy of the Word**.

## Pray with Your Family:

Lord Jesus Christ,
we are so happy that you give yourself to us at Mass.
Help us to get ready to receive you
so that we may be worthy of your gifts.
Help us respect and love
   you and all your people
   and give us joy in
   praising you.
Who live and reign with
   God the Father
in the unity of the
   Holy Spirit,
one God, for ever
   and ever.
Amen.

## To Do This Week

Think about when you go to Mass. Are you respectful of God and others at Mass? Before it starts, do you behave as if you are getting ready for something really important? What could you do better?

## Family Connection

• Read and discuss the Mass readings with your family every week. Your parish bulletin may print the Bible references for the upcoming week, or may give you another resource. You can also find the readings online at www.USCCB.org.

# Chapter 3
# We Listen to God's Word

## The Liturgy of the Word

The Word of God is alive and active. During this part of the Mass, the Word helps us learn how to be Christians and to grow in holiness. We listen to readings from the Bible that are proclaimed that day in churches all around the world. Listening to them is an important way we get ready to celebrate the Eucharist.

## Time to Listen!

God wants to talk to you (yes, you!). Though he may speak to you in prayer, he does this in a special way when you hear the words of the Bible at Mass. It is important to open your ears and your heart to hear the readings. If you do that, the Holy Spirit, who is there whenever God's Words are read aloud, will help you know what God wants you to do.

## First Reading

The reader comes to a special stand called the **ambo** and reads from a large book called the *Lectionary for Mass*, which includes the parts of the Bible that the Church wants us to hear that day.

The **First Reading**, usually from the Old Testament, tells stories of God and his people from the times before Christ was born. Many of the people we hear about in those readings are the family of Jesus Christ, and they are also part of our family of faith. During Easter Time, the First Reading is from the Acts of the Apostles and tells how people lived after Jesus Christ rose from the dead. We learn from the First Reading about God's love.

When the reader is finished, he or she says: **"The word of the Lord."** And we answer: **"Thanks be to God,"** for what we have just heard. This is followed by a short silence so we can think about what we just heard.

## Responsorial Psalm

Next, we sing the **Responsorial Psalm**. Its words come from the Book of Psalms in the Bible. The psalms are musical poems

## FuN FacT

Many psalms are attributed to King David, an ancestor of Jesus Christ, whose poems are put to music to worship God.

16

and are a prayer to God that involve our feelings —forgiveness, anger, sadness, joy, thankfulness, and praise.

First, the cantor sings the **antiphon** of the psalm. This is a short musical "sentence." Repeat it after the cantor. The cantor then sings the verses and the people sing the antiphon after each verse. Afterward, there is a short moment of silence, as we get ready to hear the **Second Reading**.

## Second Reading

The Second Reading is from letters that St. Paul and other Apostles wrote to people in Church communities around the ancient world. They wrote to teach and to answer questions about how Christ wants Christians to live. These letters help us know how to live too, so it is important to listen and learn. Because these were written a long time ago,

St. Paul

sometimes the sentences are difficult, so listen carefully. It helps if you are able to look at the readings before Mass, so your teacher or parents can help you. The priest will also help you understand what the readings mean during the **homily**. (There is usually no Second Reading at weekday Mass unless it is a special day, such as a Holyday of Obligation.)

When the reader is finished, he or she again says: **"The word of the Lord."** And we respond: **"Thanks be to God,"** for what we have just heard. Then there is more quiet time so we can think of what we just heard and get ready to hear the **Gospel**.

17

## Gospel Acclamation and Gospel

We stand to sing a special song, the **Gospel Acclamation**, to honor the reading we will hear from the Gospel writings of Matthew, Mark, Luke, or John. The Gospel is a very special reading, because it contains the words of Jesus Christ. We sing **"Alleluia!"** which means "God be praised." During Lent, we sing **"Praise and honor to you, Lord Jesus Christ"** or other special words.

The priest or deacon holds the *Book of the Gospels* high as he carries it from the altar to the ambo while we sing. Altar servers may carry lighted candles while the priest or deacon processes with the book. The priest or deacon says or sings: **"The Lord be with you."** We respond: **"And with your spirit."** The priest or deacon announces: **"A reading from the holy Gospel according to (Matthew, Mark, Luke, or John)."**

We say: **"Glory to you, O Lord,"** as we bless ourselves with three small Signs of the Cross—on our forehead, lips, and chest.

If this is a special celebration, the priest or deacon may bless

the *Book of the Gospels* with incense. We remain standing as we listen to him read the **Gospel.** When he finishes, he holds up the book and says: **"The Gospel of the Lord."** We respond: **"Praise to you, Lord Jesus Christ."** Then we sit down.

### Reflect and Share

Do you have a favorite story from the Bible that we hear at Mass? Why do you like this story? Talk about this story with your parents.

## Homily

The priest or deacon talks to us about the meaning of the readings, especially the Gospel. He may tell stories to help us know how God wants us to live. This is also a time for all of us to pay attention to what the priest or deacon is saying. After the homily is over, stay quietly seated for a few moments so you can listen inside yourself to what God is telling you.

## Creed

Next, we stand and remind ourselves of what we believe with the **Creed.** Most often we say the Nicene Creed, but sometimes we may say the shorter Apostles' Creed. Both start with **"I believe . . ."**

and tell what we believe about God the Father, Son, and Holy Spirit, one Baptism to save us from sin, one Church, and the future, when Christ will come back and we will all rise from the dead. A special part of the prayer is when we reference Christ's birth. We bow at these words. There are some big words in the Creed, especially the word **consubstantial**. This means that we believe that Christ, the Son of God, is one with the Father.

# Nicene Creed

I believe in one God,
the Father almighty,
maker of heaven and earth,
of all things visible and invisible.

I believe in one Lord Jesus Christ,
the Only Begotten Son of God,
born of the Father before all ages.
God from God, Light from Light,
true God from true God,
begotten, not made, consubstantial
    with the Father;
through him all things were made.
For us men and for our salvation
he came down from heaven,

At the words that follow, up to and including **and became man**, all bow.

and by the Holy Spirit was incarnate of the Virgin Mary,
and became man.

For our sake he was crucified under Pontius Pilate,
he suffered death and was buried,
and rose again on the third day
in accordance with the Scriptures.
He ascended into heaven
and is seated at the right hand of the Father.
He will come again in glory
to judge the living and the dead
and his kingdom will have no end.

I believe in the Holy Spirit, the Lord, the giver of life,
who proceeds from the Father and the Son,
who with the Father and the Son is adored and glorified,
who has spoken through the prophets.

I believe in one, holy, catholic and apostolic Church.
I confess one Baptism for the forgiveness of sins
and I look forward to the resurrection of the dead
and the life of the world to come. Amen.

# Apostles' Creed

I believe in God,
the Father almighty,
Creator of heaven and earth,
and in Jesus Christ, his only Son, our Lord,

At the words that follow, up to and including **the Virgin Mary**, all bow.

who was conceived by the Holy Spirit,
born of the Virgin Mary,
suffered under Pontius Pilate,
was crucified, died and was buried;
he descended into hell;
on the third day he rose again from the dead;
he ascended into heaven,
and is seated at the right hand of God the Father almighty;
from there he will come to judge the living and the dead.

I believe in the Holy Spirit,
the holy catholic Church,
the communion of saints,
the forgiveness of sins,
the resurrection of the body,
and life everlasting. Amen.

## The Universal Prayer or Prayer of the Faithful

A reader (or deacon) will then read short prayers of **intercession** for the needs of the Church, the world, people who are poor, your community, people who are sick, and those who have died. Usually, we say: **"Lord, hear our prayer."** The reader will tell you if you are to say something different. When these prayers are finished, the priest sends them to God with a special short prayer.

We have heard God's Word, which helps us know how to live the way Christ taught. As we sit down, we get ready for the **Liturgy of the Eucharist**, which helps make us holy and strong for the Christian life. We need both parts of the Mass — Word and Sacrament — to make us better disciples of Christ.

## Praying for Others

Who or what needs prayer today? With your family, take turns sharing prayers for the needs of the Church, the world, poor people, your parish community, your family, the sick, and those who have died. Finish by praying together with your family:

God our Father,
we thank you for your Word, given to us in the Bible
and for those who read to us and teach us about how to live.
Help us to listen better at Mass,
to open our hearts to what you are saying,
and to live as your holy people,
serving others and doing your will.
Through Christ our Lord.
Amen.

### To Do This Week

Listen—really listen—to the Liturgy of the Word (especially the readings and the homily) the next time you are at Mass. Were you more interested? Could you do better? What might help?

### Family Connection

- On the way home from Mass, discuss what you heard in the readings or the homily.

- What should you and your family do differently because of what you heard? How can you share this with others?

- Do you read the Bible? On your own? As a family? What might help your family to do that more often?

# Chapter 4
## We Receive Christ in the Eucharist

### Liturgy of the Eucharist

At the Last Supper, Jesus Christ turned bread and wine into his Body and Blood, sacrificed for us. He told us to do the same thing to remember him. In this part of the Mass, bread and wine will be changed, so that we, like the disciples long ago, can eat and drink Christ's Body and Blood. Around us, invisibly, we are joined by the saints, angels, and those who have died who are at God's table in heaven.

### We Get Ready: The Preparation of the Gifts

Now we "set the table" for our meal with Christ. The **Preparation of the Gifts** begins with the collection of money for the poor and for the needs of the parish. Often we sing a song at this time. Join in the singing. Sometimes there may be music without words played on the piano or organ, or no music at all. If that happens, just watch what happens at the altar and pray silently.

Members of the assembly now bring the gifts of bread (usually small, round **hosts**) and wine to the altar. We offer these things as a **sacrifice**, made by human hands, to become the Body and

Blood of Christ. We give them to the priest; then he hands them to the altar servers or deacon, who in turn place them on the altar.

The priest goes to the altar and first lifts up the **paten** with the bread, then the **chalice** of wine and offers them to God. If there is no music, he may pray this ancient prayer out loud: **"Blessed are you, Lord God of all creation, for through your goodness we have received this bread/wine we** offer you . . . " Your response is: **"Blessed be God for ever,"** each time.

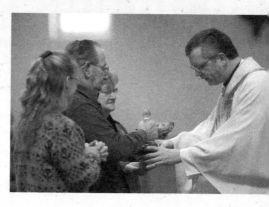

As the priest lifts up the bread and wine, silently ask God to accept your life as an offering along with the gifts of bread and wine. God wants you to help make the world a better place by obeying his will.

Then, we stand up. The priest asks us to pray that God may accept our **sacrifice**. Our response is: **"May the Lord accept the sacrifice at your hands for the praise and glory of his name, for our good and the good of all his holy Church."**

Each week the priest reads a different prayer from *The Roman Missal* over the offering of bread and wine, again asking God to accept them. This prayer is called the Prayer over the Offerings. We say: **"Amen."** After this prayer, the **Eucharistic Prayer** begins.

## The Eucharistic Prayer

*Eucharist* means "giving thanks." Think of what you are thankful for — family, friends, your home, for example — as well as for Christ, who saves you from sin and wants to be your friend.

We give thanks to God with a special **dialogue** prayer called the Eucharistic Prayer. It has parts that are said by the priest and by the people, in the same way that two people have a conversation.

### We Offer the Sacrifice

The priest chooses one of four main Eucharistic Prayers (or some others for special occasions) from *The Roman Missal*. The parts of the Eucharistic Prayer are always the same:

- We give thanks.
- We praise God.
- The priest calls down the Holy Spirit to change the bread and wine and us.
- We hear how Christ gave us the Eucharist.
- We remember Christ's Passion, Resurrection, and Ascension.
- We offer Christ's sacrifice — and our lives — to the Father.
- We pray for the living and the dead.
- We say Amen.

### Reflect and Share

Talk with your parents about why you think we kneel after the Preface and through the Eucharistic Prayer.

### Preface and Sanctus

The Eucharistic Prayer begins with a **Preface.** Like the introduction of a book, the Preface tells us about how Christ saved us. The Preface is different for each day of the liturgical year. It begins with a dialogue between us and the priest.

The priest begins: **The Lord be with you.**

**We answer:**     And with your spirit.

Then, he says:     **Lift up your hearts.**

**We say:**     We lift them up to the Lord.

(This means we offer our hearts to God.)

| He says: | Let us give thanks to the Lord our God. |
| **We answer:** | It is right and just. |

(This means giving thanks to God is our duty as his people. It's what we do.)

At the end of the **Preface,** the priest puts his hands together and we praise God by singing the **Sanctus,** the Holy: **"Holy, Holy, Holy Lord God of hosts . . . "**

> **FUN FACT**
> *Hosts* means
> "an army of angels."

In the Sanctus we join with the angels to praise God. We sing **"Hosanna"** — a special way to say "God saves." The people shouted this word when Christ rode into Jerusalem on Palm Sunday. Then we all kneel.

### Calling Down the Spirit

Holding his hands with his palms down over the bread and wine, the priest asks the Holy Spirit to change them into the Body and Blood of Christ. He makes the Sign of the Cross over the gifts of bread and wine. He also prays for the Holy Spirit to change us, so that we can serve Christ in

the world — at home, at school, and at play. When we receive Christ in Holy Communion, we become more like him.

### Telling the Story

The priest then helps us remember Christ and his disciples at the Last Supper. The priest uses Christ's words to his disciples before he died that the bread and wine were his own Body and Blood, broken and shared for many people. This is the **institution**

**narrative**, or the words of **consecration**. The ordinary bread and wine that we have offered are now the Eucharist, the Body and Blood of Christ. The priest then sings or says: **"The mystery of faith,"** and we sing or say one of three Memorial Acclamations to remember Christ and that he will come back at the end of time. One that you may hear

often is: **"When we eat this Bread and drink this Cup, we proclaim your Death, O Lord, until you come again."**

### Remembering

As the prayer continues the priest reminds us that we celebrate the Eucharist because Christ asked us to do this in memory of him. What do we remember? His pain and Death on the Cross, his rising again, and his going back to heaven to be with God the Father.

### Offering

We ask God the Father to accept our offering of the bread and wine (and our lives) and pray that an angel will take our prayers and offerings to God's altar in heaven.

### Intercessions

We remember both the living and the dead. We pray for the people of the Church, the bishop of our diocese, and all who serve the Church around the world. We ask that those who have died be with the saints, and that when we die we may be with them too. We all want to be at "the heavenly banquet," God's holy supper in heaven.

**Through, with, and in Christ: The Doxology**

We end the Eucharistic Prayer by offering it to the Father through the Son, in the unity of the Holy Spirit. The priest (with the deacon) holds up the paten with the Body of Christ and the chalice with the Blood of Christ, says: **"Through him, and with him, and in him, O God, almighty Father, in the unity of the Holy Spirit, all glory and honor is yours, for ever and ever."** This is called the **Doxology** and we respond by saying or singing **"Amen."** The Eucharistic Prayer is now over and the bread and wine have now become the Eucharist, so we stand to pray.

## The Communion Rite

We pray, reach out to one another to share peace, then come forward, singing with joy, to receive the Body and Blood of Christ.

### The Our Father or Lord's Prayer

We prepare to receive Christ in Communion by praying the words he taught us. We sing or say together: **"Our Father, who art in heaven . . ."** Near the end of the prayer, the priest adds: **"Deliver us, Lord, we pray, from every evil . . ."** Then we sing or say the rest of the Our Father ("For the kingdom . . .") and end with **"Amen."**

> **FUN FACT**
> Why do we call Christ the Lamb of God? Read the story of the Passover in Exodus 12.

### We Share a Sign of Peace

The priest then reminds us that Christ said: **"Peace be with you,"** when he appeared to his disciples. The priest then invites us to share the peace of Christ with one another. You should share this with the people near you, shaking their hands and saying, **"Peace be with you,"** or **"The peace of Christ."**

### The Body of Christ Is Broken

Next, the priest breaks the large **host** into pieces, reminding us of Christ's sacrifice, when his Body was broken on the Cross. The priest puts a small piece in the chalice with the Precious Blood to mix them together. While he does this, we sing or say the **Lamb of God**: **"Lamb of God, you take away the sins of the world, have mercy on us"** (at least twice); then the last time, **"Lamb of God, you take away the sins of the world, grant us peace."** Now, we kneel again.

## Invited to the Table of the Lord

The priest shows us the broken **host,** saying: **"Behold the Lamb of God, behold him who takes away the sins of the world. Blessed are those called to the supper of the Lamb."** We answer: **"Lord, I am not worthy that you should enter under my roof, but only say the word and my soul shall be healed."** The priest receives Communion, then shares it with the other ministers at the altar.

## We Receive Communion

We sing during the Communion procession. When it is your turn, join the line to the altar. Come forward in a respectful manner, with your hands folded. This is Christ, really present in the Eucharist. After the person in front of you receives, step forward and bow to the sacrament before receiving.

### TRiViA

Do you know who said, "Lord, I am not worthy that you should enter under my roof . . . ?"

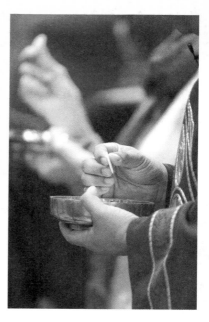

You are receiving the Body and Blood of Christ, which makes you part of his Church, also called the Body of Christ. When you say "Amen," say it like you mean it! Your Amen is your "Yes, I believe that this is really Christ," and "Yes, I am becoming part of his Body."

If you wish to receive on your tongue, open your mouth, stick out your tongue slightly, and let the priest or minister place the host on your tongue. If you receive with your hands, hold them out, with the hand you eat with on the bottom, your other hand on top. The priest or minister will place the host on your hand. Then, you may pick up the host with the hand you use to eat to put it into your mouth. Never carry the host away without eating it!

If the Precious Blood is offered, step in front of the minister holding the cup, make a slight bow, then receive the cup in both hands and take a small sip. Hand the cup back to the minister. Be careful not to bump into anyone else in line! Go back to your seat, kneel down, and start singing again.

## Saying Thank You

Back at your seat, during the quiet time after the Communion song ends, say a prayer of gratitude in your heart to Christ. You may sit after the priest sits down.

When the priest stands, stand up and listen to the **Prayer after Communion**. We ask that God will make us better people and bring us closer to him because of the Eucharist we have just received. This is now the end of the Liturgy of the Eucharist.

Imagine you have just received Communion and it's time to pray afterwards. How can you show Christ your appreciation? What would you say to him in your prayer? Draw or describe your response below.

## Pray with Your Family:

Father,
we thank you for sending your Son to save us.
We thank you for the gift of him in our lives
especially when we receive Communion.
We ask you to help us be better people,
not thinking of ourselves first,
but sharing in your sacrifice by serving
others in your name.
Through Christ our Lord.
Amen.

## To Do This Week

Practice making a slight bow at home in front of a mirror. At Mass, remember to bow before receiving the Body of Christ and again before the Precious Blood.

## Family Connection

• How does getting family members together for a special meal, such as at a holiday, a birthday, or anniversary help your family to feel closer?

• How is Mass like a family meal? How is it different?

• What would it mean to offer your life, with all its work and struggles, as a sacrifice, along with the Eucharist (see *Catechism of the Catholic Church*, 901)?

• How can you let go of "your agenda" to allow your life to reflect God's plan?

# Chapter 5
## We Are Sent Out to the World

## Concluding Rites

Mass has ended. But this moment is also the beginning—of your **mission** to the world!

## Important Instructions

Just like we do before we leave home for work or school, we want to check on a few things before we leave the church. In many parishes, someone may read a few announcements. This is how people will know of other events at church during the week and information about ministries.

## Asking for God's Blessing

Finally, the priest holds his hands over us and sings or says: **"The Lord be with you."** We answer: **"And with your spirit."** He makes the Sign of the Cross over the people, saying: **"May almighty God bless you, the Father, and the Son, and the Holy Spirit."** We, too, make the Sign of the Cross and respond: **"Amen."** On special days, we may be asked to bow our heads for a longer blessing, but we always end with the Sign of the Cross.

> **FUN FACT**
> The word *Mass* comes from the Latin word *missa*, which means "mission" or "sent."

## Dismissal: We Are Sent

Then, the priest (or deacon, if there is one) gives us our mission. It's a little like getting a homework assignment. He sings or says one of these:

"Go forth, the Mass is ended."
"Go and announce the Gospel of the Lord."
"Go in peace, glorifying the Lord by your life."
"Go in peace."

We answer: **"Thanks be to God."** Notice that we always answer to the command to "Go." We are not saying "goodbye" to God, but we are being *sent* to share his Good News and to live what Jesus Christ has taught us. We are thankful and happy to say "yes" to our mission.

### Reflect and Share

Why is it important to stay until the end of Mass?

Think about one thing you can do to show others that you have been sent by Jesus Christ to spread the Good News. Draw a picture or write a paragraph to show what that looks like.

## Pray with Your Family:

Loving Father,
you sent your Son to save us
and gave us the Eucharist to share in his memory.
We ask you to make us more faithful in celebrating the Mass
and to help us grow in holiness,
so that we can carry out your mission of love to the world.
Through Christ our Lord.
Amen.

## To Do This Week

Do you still have questions about the Mass? Ask your parents, a priest, or your teacher to help. You may want to look back at the chapters again or at the vocabulary words in the next section.

## Family Connection

- How is your family sent from Mass to serve?

- How can your family share the Good News of Christ with each other, friends, and other people?

- What did your family learn by reading this book?

- How has this book helped you understand the Mass better and how you are to live as Christians?

# Vocabulary

**Advent:** The four weeks of the liturgical year before Christmas Time. Its color is violet. In Advent, we wait for Jesus Christ to return again as well as the dawn of the light of his birth at Christmas.

**Alleluia:** A special word from the Hebrew language meaning "God be praised." We sing "Alleluia" before the reading of the Gospel at each Mass except during Lent.

**Altar Server:** A person trained to help the priest at Mass. Servers may be children or adults.

**Ambo:** A special pulpit or book stand where the Word of God is read at Mass.

**Amen:** Our response to prayers that means "so be it" or "I believe."

**Antiphon:** A chorus or refrain repeated between the verses of the Responsorial Psalm.

**Aspergillum:** A wand with a ball on the end, or a green branch, used to sprinkle holy water.

**Aspersorium:** A bucket for holy water used during blessings or the Sprinkling Rite.

**Book of the Gospels:** A large, beautifully decorated book that includes the words from the Gospel accounts of Matthew, Mark, Luke, and John.

**Cantor:** The musician who sings the Responsorial Psalm and leads the other songs at Mass.

**Censer:** A metal container with holes, used for lighted charcoal and incense. The priest, deacon, or sometimes an altar server swings it to make smoke come out.

**Chalice:** The special metal cup used by the priest for the wine that will become the Precious Blood of Christ.

**Collect:** A prayer at the beginning of Mass that guides our thoughts and prayers about the Mass we will celebrate.

**Communion:** Another word for the Eucharist. When we receive Holy Communion, we are receiving Christ into our own bodies. We do this together, with our family and friends, the members of our Church community, and every Catholic along with all the angels and saints and God's people in heaven.

**Consecration:** The special blessing the priest says over the bread and wine so that they become the Body and Blood of Christ.

**Consubstantial:** We say this word in the Nicene Creed. This word means that Christ is of one substance as the Father. He and the Father are one.

**Creed:** The words we say together at Mass that tell what we believe about the Father, Son, and Holy Spirit, the Church, Baptism, and the end of time. There are two Creeds, the Nicene Creed and the Apostles' Creed, which is also prayed during the Rosary.

**Dialogue:** When the priest and the people answer each other back and forth during the Mass.

**Doxology:** The invitation to the Great Amen that the priest sings or says at the end of the Eucharistic Prayer.

**Easter Time:** The fifty days from Easter Sunday through Pentecost. This is the time to celebrate the Resurrection of Christ.

**Eucharist:** The Body and Blood of Christ, which we receive under the appearance of bread and wine. It is another word for Communion.

**Eucharistic Prayer:** The long prayer that begins with the Preface and Sanctus (Holy) and ends with the Amen. During this prayer the bread and wine become the Body and Blood of Christ.

**First Reading:** A reading from the Bible that begins the Liturgy of the Word, always read from the ambo. During most of the year it is from the Old Testament. During Easter Time, the reading is from the Acts of the Apostles.

**Genuflect:** Bending down on one knee as one passes in front of the tabernacle, to give honor to Christ who is present in the Eucharist that is reserved inside.

**Gloria:** A song using the words the angels sang to the shepherds the night Christ was born. It is a song of thanks and praise to God that we sing during most Masses, except during Advent and Lent.

**Gospel:** The third and last reading of the Liturgy of the Word. The text is taken from the evangelists, Matthew, Mark, Luke, or John, and is read from the special book called the *Book of the Gospels.*

**Gospel Acclamation:** The short song we sing before the reading of the Gospel. We usually sing "Alleluia" except during Lent, when other special words are sung.

**Holydays of Obligation:** Special days besides Sundays when we should go to Mass. In the United States, these days are: Mary, the Holy Mother of God (January 1); Ascension of the Lord (during Easter Time); Assumption of the Blessed Virgin Mary (August 15); All Saints Day (November 1); Immaculate Conception of Mary (December 8); and Christmas (December 24/25).

**Homily:** A sermon or teaching based on either the readings of the day or the meaning of the liturgy or Mass. It is preached by a priest or a deacon.

**Hosanna:** A Hebrew word meaning "God saves." It was a kind of cheer people used to welcome Christ into Jerusalem on Palm Sunday. We sing it in the Sanctus (Holy).

**Hospitality:** The welcome every person should receive before and during Mass. Many parishes have special ministers to welcome people.

**Hosts:** Small flattened wafers of bread that will be consecrated to become the Eucharist. Also means an "army of angels" when sung during the Sanctus (Holy).

**Incense:** Sweet-smelling smoke made by burning a special mixture put onto lighted charcoal in a censer. Incense means our prayers, like the smoke, are going up to heaven.

**Institution narrative:** The part of the Mass when the priest tells how Christ shared bread and wine as his Body and Blood at the Last Supper with his disciples and asks us to do this in his memory.

**Intention:** A special prayer for someone or some situation. Every Mass has an intention, usually for someone who has died. Intentions are also special prayers for the Church, the world, the local community, the sick and the dead, and are read as part of the Universal Prayer. Each of us can have a personal intention for a Mass.

**Intercession:** A prayer asking for God's help for a person or a situation. These are sometimes also called "petitions." At Mass, these are the part of the Universal Prayer, or Prayer of the Faithful.

**Introductory Rites:** The beginning of Mass includes the opening procession and song, reverence of the altar, greeting of the assembly, Penitential Act and Kyrie or Sprinkling Rite, the Gloria (outside of Advent and Lent), and the Collect.

**Invocation:** Calling on God for help. We do that three times at the "Lord, have mercy" (the Kyrie) and at the Lamb of God.

**Kyrie, eleison:** Greek words that mean "Lord have mercy." The Kyrie is sung after the Penitential Act and is the form of a litany.

**Lamb of God:** A special prayer sung right before Communion. It is directed to Christ and how he takes away the sins of the world.

**Lectionary for Mass:** The large book used for the readings at Mass.

**Lent:** The forty days before the Sacred Paschal Triduum (Holy Thursday, Good Friday, Holy Saturday, and Easter Sunday). This is a season to look at our sins and try to do better, as we prepare to renew our Baptism at Easter.

**Litany:** A series of repeated petitions.

**Liturgical Year:** The calendar of seasons and special days the Church follows to celebrate Christ and the saints.

**Liturgy of the Eucharist:** The third part of the Mass. It includes the Preparation of the Gifts, the Eucharistic Prayer, and the Communion Rite.

**Liturgy of the Word:** The second part of the Mass. It includes the First Reading, Responsorial Psalm, Second Reading, Gospel Acclamation, Gospel, Homily, Creed, and Universal Prayer (Prayer of the Faithful).

**Minister:** A person who serves in a special role at Mass. Ministers include greeters and ushers, altar servers, sacristans, musicians, and extraordinary ministers of the Eucharist as well as the clergy (priests and deacons).

**Mission:** We are sent out from Mass with a mission to share the Good News of Jesus Christ. We do that by living his teachings and telling others that God loves us so much he sent his Son to die for us so we can live forever in heaven. The word *Mass* comes from the Latin word for "mission".

**Opening Song:**  The song sung during the opening procession.

**Participation:**  Being part of the action at Mass. Full participation means not just standing, kneeling, and sitting when everyone does, but also singing and saying the songs and responses at Mass.

**Paten:**  A special plate for the bread that will become the Eucharist.

**Penitential Act:**  At the beginning of Mass, we ask God for the forgiveness of sins. This helps make us worthy to pray to God the Father. For more serious sins, we still need the Sacrament of Reconciliation.

**Petitions:**  Short prayers asking for God's help that are read at the Universal Prayer. See also **intercession**.

**Prayer after Communion:**
A prayer from *The Roman Missal* read by the priest after Communion, asking God to give us the special benefits of the Eucharist we have just received.

**Preface:**  The first part of the Eucharistic Prayer, in which we give thanks. The Preface will be different for each season or special feast day of the liturgical year.

**Preparation of the Gifts:**  A time to collect money offered and to bring it forward along with the bread and wine for the Eucharist. The priest and altar servers also prepare the altar for the Eucharist.

**Procession:** A solemn "parade" from one place to another. There are five processions during Mass. The opening procession, the procession with the *Book of the Gospels*, the procession with the gifts of bread and wine, the procession of the people to Communion, and the procession of the ministers at the end of Mass.

**Processional Cross:** A special large cross designed to be carried. It is used to lead the opening procession and the procession of ministers at the end of Mass.

**Reader:** The person who proclaims the readings at Mass or other church services.

**Responses:** The people's answers to many of the prayers at Mass.

**Responsorial Psalm:** A Scripture reading from the Book of Psalms following the First Reading. The psalm is almost always sung by a cantor at Sunday Mass.

***The Roman Missal:*** A special book of prayers for the Mass used by the priest. It also includes instructions on how to celebrate the Mass.

**Sacrifice:** Giving something up and offering it to God. During the Eucharistic Prayer, as the priest offers the bread and wine as our sacrifice, we remember that Christ gave up his life on the Cross. Each one of us is also asked to give ourselves as a living sacrifice, offering ourselves so God can use us to do good.

**Sacristan:** Person who sets up everything needed for Mass and cleans the vessels after Mass.

**Sanctus:** The Holy is a song that we sing along with the saints and angels in heaven that remembers Christ's entrance into Jerusalem. It is our reminder at Mass that we remember Christ's sacrifice.

**Season:** A period of time in the liturgical year. Each season has a special meaning related to the life, Death, and Resurrection of Christ.

**Second Reading:** After the Responsorial Psalm at weekend Mass, we hear a reading from the Bible from the letters of Paul and the other Apostles. There is no Second Reading at daily Mass unless it is a special day.

**Sign of the Cross:** The blessing with which Catholics begin and end all prayer, including Mass: tracing a large cross over our bodies as we say, "In the name of the Father, and of the Son, and of the Holy Spirit."

**Sprinkling Rite:** A reminder of the waters of our Baptism, used as a blessing of the people instead of the Penitential Act, usually during Easter Time.

**Tabernacle:** A special cabinet for the extra consecrated hosts (the Body of Christ) that are reserved for the sick and homebound who are unable to come to Mass. It is also a place for prayer.

**Vessels:** Special plates, bowls, cups, chalices, and pitchers used for the celebration of Mass.

**Worship Aid:** A hymnal or program with the music and responses of the Mass so that you can follow along and participate.

# FROM MASS TO MISSION

### Understanding the Mass and Its Significance for Our Christian Life

## for Children

Every Sunday, we go to Mass to pray with our family, friends, and members of our parish. At Mass we worship God, giving him thanks and praise for all that he has done for us. We hear his Word, receive the Body and Blood of Christ in Communion, and are charged with an important mission — to be like Christ in the world. This booklet explains the meaning of the Mass and will help you understand why going to Mass on Sunday is so important for our Christian life.

### You will learn:

- The parts of the Mass
- Why we stand, kneel, sing, and listen
- The prayers, responses, and acclamations
- What Catholics believe about Christ
- How Mass helps us be more like Christ

*From Mass to Mission* may be used with children from grades three to six in the classroom and at home.

© Tom Quinlan

JOYCE DONAHUE serves as Catechetical Associate in the Diocese of Joliet (IL) Religious Education Office, supporting parish leaders forming adults and children. She is the author of articles published in *Pastoral Liturgy* and *Ministry & Liturgy* magazines, as well as on the *Catechist's Journey* blog. Her website is theliturgicalcatechist.weebly.com.

LTP

LITURGY
TRAINING
PUBLICATIONS

ISBN 978-1-61671-298-3

9 781616 712983

FMMC